YOUR KNOWLEDGE HA:

Bibliographic information published by the German National Library:

The German National Library lists this publication in the National Bibliography;
detailed bibliographic data are available on the Internet at http://dnb.dnb.de .

Imprint:

Copyright © 2015 GRIN Verlag, Open Publishing GmbH
Print and binding: Books on Demand GmbH, Norderstedt Germany
ISBN: 978-3-668-10797-7

This book at GRIN:

http://www.grin.com/en/e-book/311741/improving-intrusion-detection-in-manets-
researching-systems-in-mobile

Andy Reed

Improving Intrusion Detection in MANETs. Researching Systems in Mobile Ad Hoc Networks

GRIN Publishing

GRIN - Your knowledge has value

Since its foundation in 1998, GRIN has specialized in publishing academic texts by students, college teachers and other academics as e-book and printed book. The website www.grin.com is an ideal platform for presenting term papers, final papers, scientific essays, dissertations and specialist books.

Visit us on the internet:

http://www.grin.com/

http://www.facebook.com/grincom

http://www.twitter.com/grin_com

Improving intrusion detection in MANETs (Mobile Ad hoc Networks)

Table of Contents

Abstract

This paper investigates the rise in popularity of MANETs (Mobile Ad Hoc Networks) and discusses their valuable role in all manner of situations that require a rapid deployment, and a highly flexible and dynamic approach to mobile networking. The paper examines the advantages, along with the limitations of MANETs, and identifies many of the current security concerns. Examining these concerns has exposed DoS attacks as being of high priority when planning for, and provisioning a secure network. The role of the IDS has been identified as being a crucial element in the security requirements. However, it has also been identified that the IDS is not a single solution, and that there are a number of options available, each suited to a particular scenario. Many of the IDS solutions have been identified as being complex and difficult to administer and maintain, and can lead to aggressive resource consumption.

In conclusion to this paper it is felt that there is further work to be done to `develop a low resource intensive node based IDS design methodology to help protect MANET nodes from DoS attacks'.

Introduction

The ubiquitous nature of mobile communications means that connecting to the home, corporate or cellular network for many has now become a common occurrence, and in many situations even essential. The growth of 802.11 wireless networking along with 3&4G fixed cell mobile communications is evident, and widely publicised. Snyder (2012) discussed the growth of wireless technologies and identified the importance of harnessing the vast potential within this area of technology, such as in education, news and media, military, automotive, also medical applications, such as in-body communications. Snyder (2012) also states that 'wireless technology is one of the fastest growing technologies that are being implemented by various industries`.

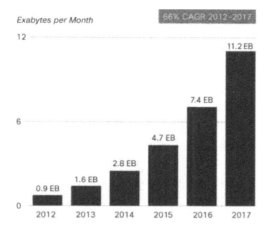

Figure 1: Growth in Mobile data traffic. (Cisco 2013)

Cisco (2013) predicts a 66% growth in mobile data traffic from 2012 to reach 11.2 Exabytes by 2017; this predicted growth can be seen in figure 1. This is growth so far is reported as being a `13 fold increase on 2012'. The white paper does identify that 41% of the 11.2 Exabytes of mobile data traffic will be consumed by Asia Pacific (APAC) users, and 18.7% by North American users. Cisco (2013) identifies that a major factor in the growth of mobile data traffic will be largely due to the increased availability, and the lower cost of mobile devices. Figure 2 shows the relationship between this predicated mobile data traffic consumption and the percentage of mobile devices that are predicted to consume the data.

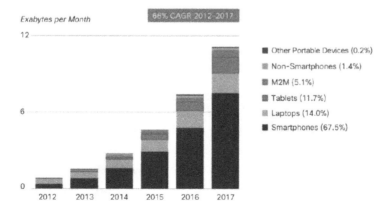

Figure 2: Data consumption by device. (Cisco 2013)

3

The mobile devices required to allow the user to connect to mobile networks are easily accessible, relatively inexpensive and easy for the end user to operate. Many organisations now allow users to access the network via personal mobile devices, this allows employees and visitors the flexibility to access documents, keep up to date with appointments, check emails and even make VoIP calls. This suggests a new paradigm in the way organisations are allowing employees to connect to the corporate network. This new shift in working practices brings with it new challenges for the security planners and network administrators. Allowing employees to access the corporate network via their own mobile device could have the potential to cause disruption to the network, introduce malware, or even result in a breach of the organisation's data protection agreement. PWC (2013) reported that 9% of large organisations were subject to a data or security breach in the last year; these breaches were a result of smart phones and table PC accessing the corporate network. The report suggests that many organisations are falling behind on the issue of securing employee owned mobile devices when accessing the network, the report also identifies that one third of small businesses have not thought about mobile security. The survey also identifies security concerns relating to mobile devices and the increasing use of BYOD (Bring Your Own Devices). Deloitte (2013) conducted a survey of 120 large organisations with the aim of gathering data on current security considerations and concerns. The results show that there has been 74% increase in the use of BYODs, and that this will only continue to grow. The report also states that the increase in BYODs has caused considerable 'security headaches' and suggested that the organisational security is becoming difficult to manage and these user devices are beginning to blur the traditional security boundaries. From this it would be safe to assume that there is much to be studied and learned about this shift in paradigm and that network and security administrators should have a sound understanding of threats posed from intentional and unintentional security breaches on both the wired and wireless network infrastructure.

Security Concerns in Mobile Networking

Network security is now very high on the agenda of any organization with an ICT infrastructure. Chan Tin (2010) stated that 'some' newspapers had reported that a number of gambling website owners have been paying blackmailers not to attack and bring down their servers. Unfortunately Chan-tin made no reference to identify the sources that were said to be the recipients of these blackmail attempts. Prolexic (2013) released an article stating that that a number of organisations that own online gambling sites have been subject to blackmail attempts. The perpetrators of the blackmail attempts were reported to have demanded up to $50,000 to prevent 'new waves' of DoS attacks from bringing down the online gambling sites. The blackmailers are reported to have used a version of the Dirt-Jumper DDoS Toolkit to carry out attacks on the gambling servers. This does appear to highlight the fact that, although DoS attacks have been around quite a while in terms of networked communications, they may still pose a significant threat to organisations that have an online presence. DoS attacks on wired networked systems have been well documented since the 1980's, with that, mitigation strategies for the numerous variants of DoS attacks have also been documented. The threat of a DoS attack is no longer solely in the domain of the wired network, DoS attacks are now known to pose a significant threat to mobile IP communications. Lee et al (2007) discussed the potential of a DoS attack faced by 3G mobile handsets. The vulnerability was identified as existing at the control plane of 3G devices, and as this is a lower level feature of the operating system architecture, Lee et al (2007) suggest that this type of DoS attack, referred to as a signalling attack will bypass current intrusion detection devices.

The growth in demand for wireless connectivity as an adjunct to the traditional wired network infrastructure shows no sign of abating, nor does the demand for more flexibility and mobility. With the popularity of BYOD (Bring Your Own Devices) and cloud computing we are now starting to see challenges for the network administrator, challenges from within the network boundary. Patrolling and controlling what goes on at the network edge is now only part of the process of securing the network. Dearing (2013) highlighted this by suggesting that the 'urgency concerning the ability to effectively monitor what is happening inside the bounds of the network is growing rapidly'.

The rise in popularity of mobile communications has seen an increase in the use and deployment of 802.11 Wireless Local Area Networks (WLANs). The popularity of WLANs can be attributed to the relatively low cost and ease of deployment. An important consideration when discussing security in the context of wireless networks is that most WLANs are merely extensions to the wired infrastructure adding flexibility and mobility. Arockiam & Vani (2010) indicated that 'one of the major attacks 802.11 WLANs face is DoS attacks'. The empirical evidence supporting this claim came from carrying out a number of experiments in a WLAN environment. The results of the experiments showed that Wireless devices were susceptible to disassociation flooding and deauthentication DoS attacks. Mölsä (2005) stated that DoS attacks are a far more serious threat to mobile ad-hoc networks than they are to wired networks. This is identified as being mostly due to the complexities of the dynamic network topology and the open architecture associated with MANETs. Mölsä (2005) also identifies DoS attacks on military mobile communications, the type of DoS attacks discussed were associated with mobile routing protocols, and states that these 'sub-types' of DoS attacks are among the most widely researched. The forwarding and routing processes on many devices that run routing protocols are carried out at the control plane. It had been seen in (Lee et al 2007) that low level attacks that occur at the control plan are difficult for IDSs to detect. The survey on security breaches carried out by (PWC 2013) identified that 39% of large companies had experienced a DoS attack, which was up 30% from the previous year. Although, these figures are not identified as relating directly to wired or wireless breaches, it does suggest that DoS attacks on organisations are on the increase. Also from the survey results it can be seen that large organisations do place more emphasis on security that SMEs.

There has been much written about the subject of wireless technologies in the popular media, and as this paper has so far proven, the use of mobile devices being used to connect to the home, work or 3/4G service provider networks show no sign of slowing down. The numerous popular technology publications, both online and on the magazine stands are starting to report on well known security issues relating mobile devices, and many are offering the user guidance on how to protect their home wireless network, or their mobile device. However, there is little written in the popular technology press on the subject of MANETs (Mobile Ad-Hoc Networks) which is now starting to mature as a mobile communications technology. The remainder of the paper will look at MANETs, the importance and growth of MANETs, along with security concerns and any the mitigation strategies that are available.

MANETs

There is a relatively new, but very important development in mobile communications that does not receive as much public attention as say 3/4G or 802.11 networks. MANETs (Mobile Ad-Hoc Networks) have been developed to work in the most remote and inhospitable environments on the planet, either on land, sea or air, areas where other wireless technologies would not be able operate effectively. The fact that MANETs are not as fixed in the public domain as its wireless counterparts should not detract from the importance of MANETs.

MANETs are self-configuring communications networks that can be used in search and rescue situations, for military applications, and for commercial and education environments. The importance of wireless communications in disaster situations was highlighted in the immediate aftermath of the 9/11 terrorist attack on the world trade centre (Malone 2004). On the night of September 11th 2001 the WERT (Wireless Emergency Response Team) was setup in an effort to coordinate and centralise the rescue effort, as the communications between emergency services, rescue workers and survivors trapped at the site were mostly by way of one-to-one cellular connections.

MANETs differ from fixed wireless infrastructures such as cellular and wireless LAN (Local Area Network) extensions in that each end device, referred to as the node, can act as a transmitter, receiver, repeater and router. Each node is mobile and is free to roam in and around the network. Each node must be able to administer its own resources such as power management, memory, routing information and security services. Torres et al (2012) discussed the 'finite resources' of MANET nodes in rescue and emergency scenarios, and identified the importance of carefully managing these resources. The authors also discussed the need for continuity in communications throughout the network, even more so when deployed in military or search and rescue scenarios where the safety and well-being of individuals is at stake.

Security Concerns with MANETs

So far this paper has looked at the growth in mobile communications and identified that there is strong evidence that like their wired counterparts, mobile communications technologies are still susceptible to DoS attacks. In this paper it has been proven that the threat of DoS attacks are of major concern to organisations, especially were websites, server and WAPs are concerned. However, when one considers the mission critical nature of a MANET node in, for instance, a medical, military or search and rescue application it is clear to see that a successful DoS attack carried out on a MANET node could have could have disastrous or even fatal consequences. The remainder of this paper will focus on security concerns associated MANETs and in particular DoS attacks.

MANETs by their design and configuration are considered more susceptible to attacks than their wired counterparts. As with any network design, thorough consideration should be given to providing security services that attempt to ensure availability, authentication, confidentiality, integrity and non-repudiation (Bhaya & Alasada 2011). The taxonomy of attacks on MANETs can be divided into two distinct categories, namely passive attacks and active attacks (Sharma & Bhadana 2010). Table 1 identifies a number of examples of security threat and classifies them as either active for passive types of attack.

Active Attacks	DoS, Spoofing, Worm Hole, Jamming, Rushing and modification.
Passive Attacks	Traffic analysis and Eavesdropping.

Table 1: Passive and Active attacks. (Sharma et al 2011)

Passive attacks occur when transmissions are covertly intercepted by a rogue node, generally with the intension of gathering important information such as sensitive data, usernames and passwords, or data relating to the physical or logical topology of the network. Active attacks are conceived to cause disruption to the operation of the network in a much more overt manner. Active attacks can cause noticeable disruptions on normal operations of services or processes, force the overuse of bandwidth or node resources, and even cause instability in the routing protocols used. There has been much written on the subject of security concerns associated with MANETs, and a large proportion of the published works on the subject covers network layer issues such as security relating to the various routing protocols available for use in MANETs. In table 2 a number of threats to MANETs have been identified, these threats have been linked to a corresponding layer of the OSI model; this indicates that MANETs have vulnerabilities spanning the seven layer of the OSI model. The table does not contain a complete list of threats to MANETs as there are many more that could be discussed. The threats contained in the table represent only a sample set as there are a number of other threats and also, quite a few variations on a theme.

Threat	Description	OSI Layer
Device Theft	Unlike other network infrastructures, a node falling into the wrong hands can give access to sensitive data such as routing information, authentication keys, and give a platform to launch other exploits on the network.	Physical layer
Jamming Attack	The propagation of excessive radio signals on the medium could cause nodes to become unavailable, effectively creating a DoS attack on the MANET node.	Physical layer
Traffic Analysis	Frame interception could allow a rogue node to gather important data on the state of the network infrastructure, traffic patterns and route information. The data gathered could be used to escalate to a more aggressive active attack.	Data Link layer
Black Hole Attack	This can occur when a rogue node advertises a link through itself to a destination node, however when the rogue node receives a packet no forwarding occurs. The rogue node drops the packet into a black hole.	Network layer
Rushing Attack	OD (On Demand) routing protocols can be susceptible to rushing attacks due to the process of route discovery used. A rogue node can overload a target node with erroneous route requests causing the target to slow down or cease processing legitimate route requests.	Network layer
Resource Depletion Attack	The rogue node can flood the network with erroneous data packets causing nodes to use up the finite resources available to them, such as memory, CPU cycles or battery power.	Network layer

TCP SYN Flooding	An attack that originated in the early 1990s has been identified as being a threat to MANETs. The attack exploits the mechanism used by TCP when forming a TCP session establishment between two nodes.	Transport layer
Session Hijacking	An exploit that takes advantage the session establishment used by TCP. The rogue node may be capable of spoofing the ID of a legitimate source node, thus taking control of the session by impersonating a legitimate node.	Transport layer
Malware Attack	As in wired and wireless networks, MANET nodes may be susceptible to malicious code such as worms, viruses, Trojan horses or spyware.	Application layer

Table 2: Threats to MANETs

Threats and Countermeasures

There are also variations of some of the threats identified in the table, for instance signal jamming is a generic term as there are a number of types of jamming attack. The physical layer can be affected by a jamming attack, this is as one would expect as the jamming is caused by signal pollution. However the MAC sub-layer of the data link layer is also susceptible to a jamming attack by manipulating the 802.11 MAC frames. Ben-Othman and Hamieh (2009) discussed signal jamming and differentiated the threat into four distinct categories, which are:

- **Constant Jammers:** The attacker continually emits RF signals in order to disrupt the normal operation on the network.
- **Deceptive Jammers:** The attacking node consecutive transmits legal frame which contain spurious content in the data filed, this forces other nodes to listen until transmission space becomes available.
- **Random Jammers**: Unlike continuous RF flooding the device can be configured to propagate RF signals at t_i time frame, and then enter a sleep state for t_s time frame. Both t_i and t_s can either variable or fixed values.
- **Reactive Jammers**: The jamming of medium when no nodes are transmitting is inefficient; a reactive jammer can listen to the medium and transmit RF signals only when other nodes are transmitting.

In order to mitigate jamming attacks it is possible to initiate channel switching strategies or set threshold values on the transmitting nodes, the values could be used to identify legitimate and MNs (malicious nodes). Ben-Othman and Hamieh (2009) discussed these options and concluded that while switching channels was a useful solution; this had little effect if the jamming node has the ability to sweep channels.

The many of the threats identified in table 2 have the potential to cause DoS (Denial of Service) attacks, having said that it could be viewed that any of these threats are no less important as they all have the potential of reducing an organisations' capacity to provide confidentiality, integrity and authentication, which make up the core components required for a secure system or network.

Much of the recent published work on MANET security does however look at the problem of DoS, and looks at a number of practical solutions to mitigate these threats. Yi et al (2010) identified a number of insecurities with network layer protocols and attributed these 'vulnerabilities' to the factors such as the open medium and the dynamic changing topologies. The threats discussed in table 2, are by no means an exhaustive list, although many of the other known security threats are, as mentioned previously, variations on a theme. For instance threats associated with the application layer, such as malware will come in many forms. These could be in the form of viruses, Trojan horses, worms or even spyware. These types of threats, while widely documented in the context of wired networks including their wireless extensions, appear to have attracted much less attention with regards to MANETs. Cole and Phamdo (2005) discussed the potential threat of a worm attack on mission critical military MANETs, and by simulating an environment where a worm was allowed to propagate the network, they concluded that the (then) current mitigation strategies at best only served to assist the propagation of the worm. The report also concluded that they had observed a ʻsubtle interplayʼ between the worm, the mitigation used and the network environment. It was suggested that to understand the nature of a worm attack on a MANET much more work is needed to be carried out. Referring back to the threats indicated in table 2 another interesting point arises, and that is that a good deal of the known threats appear to be associated with the network layer, this raises the question, are protocols or processes at the network layer of MANETs more susceptible to attacks? The issues of network layer attacks and mitigation strategies were reported in (Mantha & Sharma 2010) where it was stated that 'the foremost security issue in MANETs is to protect the network layer from malicious attacks.

Routing for MANETS

A noticeable outcome from reviewing the current published research on security threats associated with MANETs is that the network layer and in particular routing protocols have received a great detail of attention. Rajabhusanam et al (2011) discussed the problems of securing on-demand routing protocols from rogue nodes and identified this as 'an important and challenging issue.

When discussing mobile communications technologies there is one clear area that differentiates MANETs from other technologies and this is the requirement to find a feasible path to any other node on the network without the assistance of an intermediary device such a WAP, or a wireless mesh router. To locate a remote node on the network requires all MANET nodes need to have the capability to calculate, and in most cases propagate route information to all node on the network. Wired networks have the ability to use static routing, dynamic routing or a mixture of both, however due the every changing topology of MANETs; static routing is not an appropriate solution. Static routing requires the manual configuration of all routes to each network segment or subnet. This fixed configuration of all reachable subnets on the network is a very useful, relatively easy to maintain, and a low overhead solution for small network environments where routes are fixed and are unlikely to change. For networks where nodes are constantly changing location and distance from each other static routing is not a feasible solution. The mobility and flexibility of MANETs requires routing processes that will create and maintain a constant path to every node on the network, or be able to quickly find a path through the network to the destination node. Dynamic routing protocols have been around for a long time in the wired network environment, IGPs (Internal Gateway Protocols) such as EIGRP (Enhanced Interior Gateway Routing Protocol), RIP (Routing Information Protocol), ISIS (Intermediate System to Intermediate System) and OSPF (Open shortest Path First) are all proven and time served protocols. These dynamic routing protocols are used by organisations to build and maintain databases, and routing tables in order to route traffic efficiently to the destination network. The dynamic nature of these protocols makes them ideal propositions for the routing requirements of MANETs. In fact most of the routing protocols developed for MANETs are based on these well-known IGPs.

In order for a MANET node to identify a path to a remote node there needs to be a method of establishing, maintaining, and removing if required, routes to every node in the network. This can be achieved by each node creating a graph G, with vertices v and edges e. Where each vertex v represents a node and each edge e represents a path to a remote node, this gives an un-weighted graph of G(v,e).

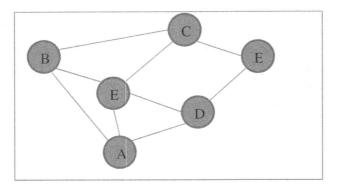

Figure 3: Un-weighted Graph.

Due to the distance limitations where nodes may move out of range, nodes may not be able to become adjacent to every other node. In figure 3 each node A, B, C, D, E has a path to every other node, although it can be seen that not all nodes are adjacent. For instance node A has a path to nodes C and E, but is not adjacent to C and E as these nodes may be out of range, but are still installed in the routing table. It can also be seen that for A to get to C and E there are a number of possible paths that can be taken, it is the role of the routing protocol algorithm to calculate the best path. The type of protocol used dictates how the best path to the remote node is calculated, for instance the number of nodes or hops, along the path will be considered by a DVRP (Distance Vector Routing Protocol), or a value could be used to give each link a weight, or cost. This method of calculating the cumulative cost of a link is found in LSRPs (Link State Routing Protocols). In reality the weight of a link can be calculated by including one or more, or a combination of the following:

- The cost of a link.
- The delay experienced on the link.
- The reliability of the link.
- The available bandwidth of the link.
- The overall load of the link.

Many of the routing protocols proposed as solutions for routing in MANETs consider these listed factors for route selection, these factors are commonly referred to as metrics. Also it will be seen that these DVRPs and LSRPs are often re-worked versions of traditional wired routing protocols in order create a routing protocol that can thrive in the often chaotic network environments found in MANETs.

Routing Protocols

The numerous routing protocols used in MANETs have been and are still the subject of much research. The architecture, mobility and the constraints placed on nodes makes for an extremely challenging topic. However, there are a number of proposed routing protocols which Sarker et al (2012) states can be placed into three distinctive categories, which are:

- Proactive routing protocols.
- Reactive routing protocols.
- Hybrid routing protocols.

The definitions are derived from the way in which a routing protocol gathers and maintains routes to remote nodes. Proactive routing protocols, sometimes referred to as table driven protocols maintain a table of routes at all nodes at all times. Most of the proactive routing protocols have inherited some of the features found in routing algorithms, for instance OLSR (Optimised Link state Routing) is based on the traditional LSRP, but has been 'tailored for mobile ad-hoc networks' (Clausen & Jacquet 2003). As the routing table is constantly kept up to date this is said to incur more overhead than reactive routing protocols (Sarker et al 2012).

Reactive routing protocols, also known as on-demand routing protocols do not keep a constant table of all routes, instead these protocols can discover the routes as and when required. A route is only calculated when a connection is required, and as such this type of protocol will need to flood the network with a route request in order to find the best path to the remote node. This process of flooding the network with route requests can incur delay sending and receiving packets from the source to the destination nodes. The AODV (Ad-hoc On-demand Distance Vector) routing protocol is an example of a reactive routing protocol, this is a variation of the traditional DVRP which considers the hop count at the metric, and can use either unicast or multicast packets to build the routing table.

In the hybrid routing protocols some of the best features of reactive and proactive routing protocols are used to create routing protocols that can operate more efficiently in a hierarchical topology. Sarker et al (2012) discussed how hybrid protocols such as ZRP (Zone Routing Protocol) and ZHLS (Zone-based Hierarchical Link state) have been developed to allow minimised routing overhead on nodes by partitioning the network into zones.

The performance of proactive, reactive and hybrid routing protocols was analysis from a number of experiments using the network simulator NS2, the results from these experiments in (Babaiyan and keshtgari 2012) showed that of the three types of routing protocol the hybrid protocol GRP (Gathering-based Routing Protocol) showed comparable performance when compared with AODV and OLSR.

Insecurities in MANET Routing Protocols

The relative immaturity of the routing technologies developed for MANETs does make them the subject of much research, debate and uncertainty as to the overall level of security they have. Many of the routing protocols used or proposed are in their relative infancy compared to routing protocols such as EIGRP, ISIS and OSPF. There has been much research in the area of security and vulnerabilities for MANET routing protocol, and from the numerous experiments carried out to examine vulnerabilities, as in (Von Mulert et al 2012) where by practical analysis it was proven that AODV was vulnerable to a number of attacks such as router resource depletion, route disruption and false route injection. Many of these vulnerabilities have the potential to slow down, or even prevent a node from learning routes to remote nodes or even joining the network. In a mission critical environment the impact of any of the vulnerabilities turning into an actual event could be catastrophic.

Misuse goals	Type of misuse			
	Drop: Routing or data packets are dropped without forwarding.	Modify and forward: MN incorrectly modifies routing control message and forwards it.	Forged reply: MN sends forged routing control message in response to real message.	Active forge: MN sends forged route control message without first receiving a real one.
Route disruption: Disrupting routing tables and breaking links.	Dropping RREQ, RREP or data messages.			MN broadcasts forged RERR causing other nodes to delete routes from routing table; using large DSN will cause new RREQ to appear stale and be ignored.
Route invasion: MN attracts routes to itself and packets may now be intercepted or dropped.		MN attracts routes by forging hop count or DSN in RREP to make route appear shorter or fresher.	MN impersonates destination node by sending RREP with forged destination in response to RREQ.	MN impersonates source node with forged source in RREQ.
Node isolation: Attempting to	Routing messages are forwarded	MN attracts routes through	MN impersonates destination node	Routes to a node can be disrupted

isolate a node from communicating with the rest of the network.	while data messages are dropped; known as black hole attacks	forging hop count or DSN in RREP to make route appear shorter or fresher, then drops data packets; composite misuse.	by sending RREP with forged destination in response to RREQ, then drops data packets; composite misuse.	by sending forged RERR messages. In SAODV, where the RERR messages are authenticated, an MN can only isolate itself this way.
Resource depletion: A type of Denial of service attack that attempts to use up network resources, e.g. battery power, storage space, etc.				Flooding the network with RREQs or RERRs to use up resources; sending junk data packets.

Table 3: AODV Vulnerabilities. (von Mulert et al 2012)

Von Mulert et al (2012) carried out a number of experiments to measure the potential vulnerabilities on routing in MANETS, their research chose to focus on the reactive AODV routing protocol. The results of the research suggested that AODV was susceptible to worm-hole attacks, where the attacker responds to RRQs (Route Requests) but does not forward the packets on to the destination, thus causing loss of connectivity. Also rushing attacks are discussed, this involves a MN (Malicious Node) which could flood the network with RREQs causing the target node to become overwhelmed and reducing its capacity to operate effectively. Table 3 gives a summary and short description of the some of the vulnerabilities faced by the AODV routing protocol.

A number of other routing protocols have been identified has having vulnerabilities, and there have been some research carried out in to identifying and proposing practical solutions to mitigate the exploits that these vulnerabilities may bring. Marimuthu and Krishnamurthi (2012) discussed a vulnerability faced by the proactive routing protocol OLSR. This attacks was identified as a node isolation attack, by where a node or cluster of nodes are targeted by a MN with the intention of preventing the propagation of route information, and as such isolating them for the rest of the network. This type of attack is achieved by altering the normal relay of route information by manipulating the MPR (Multipoint Relay) selection algorithm (Kannhavong et al 2006)

There does appear to be a need to discuss the issue of security in the context of the routing protocols used in MANETs. The dilemma of securing the routing protocols whilst minimising the resource consumption of nodes is one of much debate. Ahirwal and Mahour (2012) performed a number of simulated DoS attacks on nodes running the AODV routing protocol using the NS2 network simulator. The results of the simulations highlighted that under attack conditions the nodes became low on resources and were unable to process and forward packets efficiently.

The many advantages of using MANETs as a rapid deployment solution in hostile or remote environments has been identified in this paper, it has also been identified that there is significant evidence that suggests there are a number of associated vulnerabilities and security issues. These are by no means trivial, especially when one considers the situations that MANETs may well be deployed in. Malone (2004) discussed how non wired communication has become a 'critical asset' in search and rescue operations. There has been much written on the many benefits of MANETs, however as this paper has identifies, there are still concerns regarding potential attacks on MANETs and their nodes. There is a growing body of evidence that making MANETs more secure is vital, and necessary if the technology is to flourish. On the security of MANETs there has been considerable research around IDS (Intrusion Detection Systems) and IPS (Intrusion Preventions Systems). The topic of detecting malicious activity on the MANET is a fertile research area, and gaining much attention from the research community. On considering the application of IDSs and IPSs Karmore and Bodkhe (2011) considered the types of attacks faced, for instance passive and active, along with the dynamic environment and suggested that IDS would be a more practical solution in the move to add security to MANETs.

Intrusion Detection for MANETs

On looking at solutions to mitigate these attacks Yi et al (2010) discussed the use of, and challenges of deploying an IDS to help protect against attack to the network. As with traditional wired networks detecting anomalous traffic is a vital component in maintaining a secure network. In the wired infrastructure the IDS sensor can be tactically situated in the network to capture and analyse traffic. The IDS can be a dedicated module or host based solution that will have appropriate resources, and a continuous power supply. However as each node in a MANET can act as both host and router there is a need to consider placing the IDS on each node, this in turns raises concerns of aggressive resource consumption and power management issues. Also the architecture of the network will have a bearing on how and where the IDS may be deployed. In a flat architecture each node is considered as an equal peer and is responsible for route forwarding decisions, whilst in a multilayer architecture nodes may be segmented into clusters (Rafsanjani et al 2008). The multilayer architecture being more hierarchical in design allows the nodes in a cluster to communicate through a cluster head node. This is in essence similar to a hub and spoke topology found in wired network infrastructures.

A generic IDS has a number of essential functions, such as monitoring, storing, analysing and responding. The IDS can be either host based (HIDS) or network based (NIDS), the HIDS are designed to be more appropriate in detecting software, VPN exploits, malicious code or application layer attacks. A NIDS has the advantage of focusing on attacks on the physical layer up to the transport layer. Both have an important role to play in the protection of the network, and in most cases should be deployed in unison. Farhaoui et al (2011) recommended that whilst 'there is no perfectly complete system' security can be optimised with the combination of these systems. A major issue with regard to IDSs is the problem associated with the generation of false positives and false negatives, Stanciu(2013) identified these issues as being fundamental limitations, and suggested improvements were needed.

There have been a number of IDS solutions for MANETs proposed, each attempting to address the problem of securing nodes in a dynamic and ever changing network environment. Saminathan & Selvakumar (2011) proposed a trust based intrusion detection approach, called TRUCE, where each node would create a TV (Trust Value) of each neighbour node based the trustworthiness of the node. The TVs are used to detect and identify reliable nodes, which are marked as trustworthy, and to identify any 'misbehaving nodes'. Previously proposed trust based approaches, such as described in (Umuhoza et al 2007) use a fixed value, referred to as the metric to identify the trustworthiness of a node, whereas the TRUCE solution in (Saminathan & Selvakumar 2011) uses a variable TV assigned by neighbouring nodes. The TRUCE scheme simulation results suggest that by identifying and marking misbehaving nodes showed improvements in the response times on the network, however as this is termed as a 'Trust Aware Application' it may not be able to protect the node from lower layer DoS attacks such as those that the control plane. Given the transient nature of nodes in the MANET environment it could be argued that the process of building and maintaining trust based profiles for neighbours can be resource intensive. Torres et al (2012) This problem of resource consumption could also be compounded as neighbour nodes move out of direct cell range and new nodes form neighbour adjacencies.

Collaborative approaches to IDS deployment suggested for cluster based architectures are said to address the problem of resource depletion of MANET nodes. Rafsanjani (2010) discussed how cluster based solutions can be deployed in a multilayer architecture; the advantage here is that a cluster head, often referred to as the monitoring node can take over the responsibility of hosting the IDS from nodes within its cluster. This type of IDS deployment has the benefit of reducing the overhead on the link, on the nodes and also addresses the problem of aggressive power consumption. A notable disadvantage to a cluster based IDS is that it can introduce a single point of failure; this is due to the monitoring node in the cluster being the point of ingress. Another disadvantage is the complexity in managing and maintaining the election and re-election of the monitoring nodes, which can include gathering information from neighbouring nodes on power levels and distance. There does appear to be a general consensus that there is a real need to address the security concerns relating to DoS threats. Ahirwal and Mahour (2012) stated that MANETs are susceptible to DoS attacks due to their 'salient characteristics', also Rafsanjani et al (2008) concludes that MANETs are extremely vulnerable to attacks, this is attributed to the 'absence of conventional security infrastructure'. From the literature reviewed in the preparation of this paper it does appear that there is no general solution to reducing the problem of DoS attack on MANET nodes, and there is not indeed a 'one shoe fits all' solution.

Conclusion

MANETs have proven viable and practical solutions that have received a good deal of attention from the research community in recent years. The flexibility and robustness of MANETs make them ideally suited to search and rescue situations, deployment in area of civil unrest, for military applications and even for commercial and educational environment. Security in MANETs has received much attention too, and from the published material it is clear that this is receiving a lot of interest in the field of research. From evaluating some of the current research literature it is clear to see that security in MANETs is, relative to other network architectures, in its infancy. This can be seen by the array of proposed solutions to mitigate the numerous security threats faced in a MANET environment. Threats faced by MANET nodes range from the physical layer to the application layer, many of these threats focusing on the various routing protocols that are used in MANET architectures. The majority of threats appears to be active in nature, and are intended to cause disruption or lead to a DoS attack. Numerous IDS solutions have been proposed to mitigate attacks across the layers of the OSI model, many of these solutions are designed to protect the processes used by the routing protocols. Many of these IDS solutions are considered resource intensive or can create single points of failure in the network. From reviewing the research carried out so far and evaluating the existing IDS solutions, it would appear appropriate to suggest that there is a need to, 'develop a low resource intensive node based IDS design methodology to help protect MANET nodes from DoS attacks'.

References

Ahirwal, R and Mahour, L. (2012) 'Analysis of DDoS Attack Effect and Protection Scheme in Wireless Mobile Ad-hoc Network'. International Journal of Computer Science and Engineering. Vol. 4 No. 6, pp. 1164-1173

Arockiam, L. & Vani, B. (2010) 'A Survey of Denial of Service Attacks and its Countermeasures on Wireless Network'. International Journal on Computer Science and Engineering. Vol. 02, No. 05, pp. 1563-1571

Babaiyan, V. and keshtgari, M. (2012) *Performance Evaluation of Reactive,Proactive and Hybrid Routing Protocols in MANET'*. International Journal on Computer Science and Engineering. Vol. 4, No. 2, pp. 248-254

Ben-Othman, J. and Hamieh, A. (2009) *Defending Method Against Jamming Attack in Wireless Ad Hoc Networks'*. The 5th IEEE International Workshop on Performance and Management of Wireless and Mobile Networks. Vol., No., pp.758,762

Bhaya, W. and Alasadi, S. (2011) *Security against Spoofing Attack in Mobile Ad Hoc Networks'*. European Journal of Scientific Research, Vol. 64, No. 4, pp. 634-643

Chan-Tin, E. (2010) 'Distributed Denial of Service Attacks: Analysis of Defences'. Germany. VDM Verlag Dr. Muller Aktiengesellschaft & Co. KG.

Cisco. (2013) *Cisco Visual Networking Index: Global Mobile Data Traffic Forecast Update, 2012–2017'*. (Online). http://www.cisco.com/en/US/solutions/collateral/ns341/ns525/ns537/ns705/ns827/white_paper_c11-520862.html. [Accessed 01/09/2013]

Clausen, T. and Jacquet, P. (2003) *Optimized Link State Routing Protocol (OLSR)'*. (Online) IETF RFC3626. http://www.ietf.org/rfc/rfc3626.txt [Accessed 01/10/2013]

Cole, R. Phamdo, N. Rajab, M. and Terzis, A. (2005) 'Requirements on Worm Mitigation Technologies in MANETS'. Workshop on principles of advanced and distributed simulation. Monterey, California, June 2005. IEEE Computer Society, pp. 207-216

Dearing, T. (2013) 'Flow Mapped Security'. Network Computing, Vol. 22, No. 02, p. 23

Deloitte. (2013) *Blurring the lines:2013 TMT Global Security Study'*. (Online) http://www.deloitte.com/tmtsecuritystudy#. Deloitte. [Accessed 09/09/2013]

Donner, M. (2012) *'Prolexic Issues Global Warning about Recent DDoS Blackmail Attempts Targeting Online Gambling Sites'*. [Online] PRWeb. http://www.prweb.com/releases/2012/4/prweb9455636.htm (Accessed 10/09/2013)

Farhaoui, Y. and Asimi, A. (2011) `Performance Method of Assessment of the Intrusion Detection and Prevention Systems'. International Journal of Engineering Science and Technology Vol. 3, No. 7, pp. 5916-5928

Kannhavong, B. Nakayama, H. Kato, N. Nemoto, Y. and Jamalipour, A. `Analysis of the Node Isolation Attack Against OLSR-based Mobile Ad Hoc Networks'. Proceedings of ISCN'06 7th International Symposium on Computer Networks (IEEE Cat. No.06EX1429). Istanbul, 16-18 June 2006. IEEE Conference Publications, PP. 30 – 35

Karmore, P. and Bodkhe, S. (2011) `A survey on Intrusion in Ad Hoc Network and its Detection Measures'. International Journal on Computer Science and Engineering. Vol. 3, No. 5, pp. 1896-1903

Lee, et al. (2009) `On the detection of signalling DoS attacks on 3G/WiMax wireless networks'. Computer Networks, Vol. 53, No. 15, pp. 2601-2616

Mamtha, G. and Sharma, S. (2010) `Network Layer Attacks and Defence Mechanisms in MANETS- A Survey'. International Journal of Computer Applications, Vol. 9, No. 9, pp. 12-17

Malone, B. (2004) `Wireless search and rescue: Concepts for improved capabilities'. Bell labs Technical Journal, Vol. 9, No. 2, pp. 37-49

Mölsä, J. (2005) `Increasing the DoS attack resiliency in military ad hoc networks'. IEEE conference. Atlantic City, NJ; Oct 2005. IEEE.

Rafsanjani, M. (2010) `Generalised Mechanism for Intrusion Detection in Mobile Ad Hoc Network'. Indian Journal of Science and Technology, Vol. 3, No. 10 pp. 1098-1101

Rafsanjani, M. Movaghar, A and Koroupi, F. (2008) `Investigating Intrustion Detection Systems in MANETs and Comparing IDSs for Detecting Misbehaving Nodes'. Proceedings of world adademy of science, engineering and technology. Vol. 34, pp. 351-355

Rajabhusanam, C. Subramaniam, M. and Kathirvel, A. (2011) 'Burglar Detecting System for Wireless Mobile Ad Hoc Networks'. European Journal of Scientific Research, Vol. 62, No. 1, pp. 14-23

Saminathan, R. and Selvakumar, K. (2011) `TRUCE – An Adaptive Trust Management Algorithm Over MANET for Service-Based Mobile Computing Environments'. Information Security Journal: A Global Perspective. Vol. 5, No. 4/5, pp. 173-184

Sarker, K, S. Basavaraju,T, G and Puttamadappa, C. (2013) Ad-Hoc Mobile Wireless Network, 2nd Edn. Boca Raton. CRC Press.

Sharma, K. Khandelwal, M. and Prabhakar, M. (2011) `An Overview Of security Problems in MANET'. (online) http://psrcentre.org/images/extraimages/155.pdf. [Assessed on 04/10/2013]

Sharma, p. and Bhadana, P. (2010) `An Effective Approach for Providing Anonymity in Wireless sensor Network: Detecting Attacks and Security Measures'. International Journal on Computer Science and Engineering. Vol. 02, No. 05, pp. 1830-1835

Snyder, R. (2012) `Current Trend in Wireless Technology'. Global Conference on Business and Finance Proceedings. Vol. 7, No. 2, pp. 68-75

Stanciu, N. (2013) `Technologies, Methodologies and Challenges in Network Intrustion Detection and Prevention Systems'. Informatica Economica, Vol. 7, No. 1, pp. 144-156

Torres, R. Mengual, L. Marba, O. Eibe, S. Menasalvas, E. and Maza, B. (2012) `A management Ad Hoc networks model for rescue and emergency scenarios'. Expert Systems with Applications. Vol. 39, No. 10, pp. 9554–9563

Von Mulert, J. Welchn, I. and Seah, W. (2012) `Security threats and solutions in MANETs: A case study using AODV and SAODV'. Journal of Network and Computer Applications. Vol. 35, No. 4, pp. 1249–1259

Yi, P. Wu, Y. Zou, F. and Liu N. (2010) 'A Survey on Security in Wireless Mesh Networks'. IETE Technical Review, Vol. 27, No. 1, pp. 6-14

Bibliography

Kathirvel, A. Rajabhusanam, C and Subramaniam, M.(2001) `Burglar Detecting System for Wireless Mobile Ad Hoc Networks'. European Journal of Scientific Research. Vol.62, .No. 1, pp. 14-23

Kumar, S. and Sahoo, B. (2010) `Effect of Rushing Attack on DSR in wireless Mobile Ad hoc Network'. Department of Computer Science & Engineering. New York, WiSe '03 Proceedings of the 2nd ACM workshop on Wireless security.

Marsan, C, D. (2008) Morris Worm Turns Twenty: Look what it's done [Online] Available at http://www.networkworld.com/news/2008/103008-morris-worm.html (Accessed 09/05/2013)

Sani, S. (2013) `Jamming attack in MANETs', Golden Research Thoughts, Vol 2, No. 12, pp. 1-6.

www.ingramcontent.com/pod-product-compliance
Lightning Source LLC
LaVergne TN
LVHW042315060326
832902LV00009B/1508